What if we do N**O**THING?

POLLUTION

Christiane Dorion

FRANKLIN WATTS
LONDON•SYDNEY

First published in 2009 by Franklin Watts

Copyright © 2009 Arcturus Publishing Limited

Franklin Watts
338 Euston Road
London NW1 3BH

Franklin Watts Australia
Level 17/207 Kent Street, Sydney, NSW 2000

Produced by Arcturus Publishing Limited,
26/27 Bickels Yard, 151-153 Bermondsey Street,
London SE1 3HA

Series concept: Alex Woolf
Editor: Alex Woolf
Designer: Phipps Design
Picture researcher: Alex Woolf

The illustrations on pages 13, 15 and 25 are by
Phipps Design.

A CIP catalogue record for this book is available
from the British Library.

Dewey Decimal Classification Number: 363.73

ISBN 978 0 7496 8746 5

Printed in China

Franklin Watts is a division of Hachette
Children's Books, an Hachette UK company.
www.hachette.co.uk

Picture Credits
Arcturus Publishing: 7 (Adam Hook).
Corbis: cover *bottom left* (Bettmann), 4 (Liu Liqun), 6 (Roger
Wood), 8 (Hulton-Deutsch Collection), 12 (Fritz Hoffmann), 16 (Hans
Strand), 23 (Peter Turnley), 24 (Chinch Gryniewicz), 26 (Reuters),
32 (Benjamin Lowy), 34 (Mast Irham/epa), 38 (Gideon Mendel), 39
(Roger Ressmeyer), 42 (Kristy-Anne Glubish/Design Pics).
Getty Images: 18 (AFP), 43 (China Photos/Stringer), 44 (Charley
Gallay/Stringer).
Rex Features: 37 (Paul Cooper).
Science Photo Library: cover *background* (Robert Brook), 14 (P
Baeza, Publiphoto Diffusion), 20 (Gary Hincks), cover *top right* and
29 (Garry D McMichael), 31 (Jerry Mason).
Shutterstock: 10 (David Má_ka), 30 (Noam Armonn), 40 (Karen
Roach), 41 (Petr Nad).

Cover pictures
bottom left: Workers on an oil rig spray chemical dispersant on an
oil spill in the Bay of Campeche, Gulf of Mexico.
top right: A crop duster sprays insecticide on carrots near McAllen,
Rio Grande Valley, Texas.
background: Chemicals from buried industrial waste collect on the
ground surface at Heath End, West Midlands, UK.

Every attempt has been made to clear copyright. Should there be
any inadvertent omission, please apply to the publisher for
rectification.

Contents

The State of Our Planet

It is 2025. Wearing a mask to go for a walk or play football is now the norm in large cities. Water is very expensive and wars over water sources afflict many countries. More than half of the world population lives in cities. It is hard to find suitable land for new houses as so much has been contaminated by industry. Air pollution is changing the world's climate. The earth's average temperature is rising, the polar ice caps have nearly melted and floods affect many cities. How could the world believe for so many years that pollution was an acceptable part of progress?

The unwanted stuff

Pollution is the release of harmful substances into the environment by human activity. When we make and use things, we often ignore what we create unintentionally in the process. For example, to make computers, we dig out mountains to extract metals, using and creating toxic substances in the process. We use energy to transport these metals around the globe and release unwanted gases into the air. More energy is used in factories to make these computers, and more chemicals are pumped into the air and poured into rivers. We also use thousands of artificial substances, which cannot break down naturally. Instead, they build up in the environment.

Burning coal to produce electricity is a major cause of air and water pollution. This is a coal power plant in China, the largest coal producer and consumer in the world.

When old computers are dumped, toxic substances such as lead and mercury can slowly soak into the soil and find their way into the water we drink. Why do we make things this way? Because, for a long time, we thought that the planet was big enough to diffuse these substances over time. We have now reached a level of pollution that the earth can no longer absorb.

THE FIVE DIRTIEST PLACES IN THE WORLD

The following list was produced by looking at the number of people affected, the types of pollutants and their impact on people's health.

City	Country	Sources	Number of people affected
Sumgayit	Azerbaijan	Production of industrial chemicals and pesticides	275,000
Linfen	China	Cars and coal industry	3,000,000
Tianying	China	Mining and processing of lead	140,000
Sukinda	India	Mining of chromite	2,600,000
Vapi	India	Production of industrial chemicals and heavy metals	71,000

Source: Blacksmith Institute, 2007

Amazing earth

The earth is the only planet in the whole solar system with air to breathe, water to drink and temperatures that can sustain life. These amazing conditions are regulated by complex natural systems. Water continuously moves around between land, ocean and sky. The atmosphere contains the right balance of gases to support life and to protect living things from the sun's radiation.

Everything in nature is interconnected. Plants have the ability to use the sun's energy to produce food. When plants and animals die, they decompose and enrich the soil. Human activities are affecting these natural systems. By putting pressure on the environment in one place, it can affect other, often far away places in unpredictable ways.

For example, dangerous chemicals such as mercury and lead have been found in the bodies of people living in the Arctic, thousands of kilometres from any factory. The wind and ocean currents can carry industrial pollutants far from their original sources.

Not a new problem

Pollution is not new. What is new is the amount and type of pollution we produce and the impact it has on the whole planet. Our early ancestors were nomadic, hunting and moving around in search of food. They produced very little waste – mainly ash from fires and objects made out of stone, wood and bones.

The Romans were famous for their technology. These public toilets in the Roman town of Dougga, Tunisia, date from between 100 and 200 BCE. They could seat 12 people. The waste was fed through a drainage system to the town's main drain.

Their waste was biodegradable. This means that it could be broken down naturally by bacteria in the soil. In about 5,000 BCE, people discovered how to smelt copper in open fires to make tools and ornaments. Later on, bronze and iron were produced to make better tools, weapons and armour. The world population was very small and these activities left a tiny amount of waste without too much impact on the environment.

Ancient world

Pockets of pollution began to appear as communities grew larger and villages developed into towns and cities. The major civilizations of the ancient world emerged in Mesopotamia, Egypt, India, China, Persia, Greece and Rome. These peoples forged metal on a large scale and used water power to make things. They burned wood and peat as fuel for cooking and heating.

The Romans made important advances in engineering. They built sewers to remove human waste and set up a system of rubbish collection. They built aqueducts to supply water to cities, and pipes to bring fresh water into their homes. Although their cities were fairly clean, Roman mining and smelting of metals caused pollution. Scientists have even found traces of lead pollution in the ice of Greenland, which came all the way from Roman smelters. Yet most of this early pollution was local and limited in its effects on the environment.

Middle Ages

In medieval Europe, urban pollution increased. Towns and cities were overcrowded, noisy and dirty places. Rubbish and waste from butchers, dyers, and other trades were often thrown straight into the street, along with human waste. People were not aware of the link between dirty water and the spread of disease.

Wood was the major source of fuel during ancient and medieval times. Due to the needs of an expanding population, the forests began to recede in Europe, and coal became increasingly important for cooking, heating and powering machinery. By the 15th century, many European cities were polluted by coal smoke.

In medieval towns, people would tip the contents of their chamber pots out of the window into the streets, which had open drains. The usual warning cry was 'Gardez l'eau', French for 'watch the water'.

In 1661 the British scientists John Evelyn and John Graunt argued that air pollution could affect plants, wildlife and people. They suggested moving factories to the countryside and using taller chimneys to reduce the effects of pollution. But many tradesmen were reluctant to give up their prime spots by rivers and near major market places.

Industrial Revolution

Pollution increased dramatically when the Industrial Revolution began in Britain in the late 18th century, spreading to mainland Europe and North America in the 19th. The invention of power-driven machinery prompted the move away from small workshops producing handmade goods to large-scale factory production. Industrial cities became polluted with the fumes from factory chimneys. The factories needed energy to

PRODUCTION OF COAL IN BRITAIN	
1700	2.7 million tonnes
1750	4.7 million tonnes
1800	10 million tonnes
1850	50 million tonnes
1900	250 million tonnes

Source: www.historylearningsite.co.uk

Cities like London developed rapidly in the 19th century. This 1872 engraving by Gustave Doré shows the overcrowded and poor living conditions in London's East End.

drive the machines. This was provided by burning coal. Coal was also used to heat the homes of city-dwellers. This greatly added to air pollution. Smog – a mixture of smoke and fog – was common in large cities such as Paris and London. In winter, cool air would rise from the river and mix with coal smoke from millions of chimneys to form a thick black fog.

Untreated sewage and industrial waste were often dumped in rivers. By the mid-1800s, water pollution in major cities had become a serious problem. The River Thames, the main source of drinking water for London, became a cesspool of human waste from nearly 3 million people. Diseases carried by rats and fleas were common and epidemics of cholera and typhoid decimated towns and villages across Europe. Scientists began to understand the link between water pollution and outbreaks of disease. In the 1850s, sewers were built in European and North American cities to divert human waste to rivers and seas.

SERIOUS EPISODES OF SMOG

When?	Where?	Why?	Impact
1892	London, UK	Burning of coal, and fog	Death of 1,000 people
1948	Donora, Pennsylvania, USA	Toxic gases from zinc smelting plant, and fog	Death of 20 people and thousands hospitalized
1952	London, UK	Burning of coal, and fog	Death of 4,000 people

Source: www.enviropedia.org.uk

Modern world

During the 20th century, the world's population rose dramatically. Manufacturers developed new products to appeal to a growing class of wealthy consumers. Cars, radios, televisions and domestic appliances were among the most popular products of the early 20th century. Manufacturers brought out new ranges of products each year. By clever marketing, they persuaded customers that what they had bought the previous year was now out of date. This attitude helped increase pollution levels as perfectly good products were discarded in favour of the latest model.

From the 1940s, new products were developed, including plastics, synthetic fabrics and dyes, antibiotics and pesticides, which improved the lives of millions of people. However, many of these substances do not decompose naturally and instead build up in the environment.

Nuclear power, also developed in the 1940s, promised a new, cheap source of energy. But it brought with it the problem of radioactive waste, which remains dangerous for thousands of years.

In the later 20th century, countries such as China, India and Brazil embarked on massive industrialization programmes. This led to a major increase in pollution from cars, factories, mines and farms. The lower labour costs of the newly industrialized nations meant that goods could be sold more cheaply, fuelling a boom in retail sales. As prices fell for products such as clothing and electronic goods, consumers were encouraged to throw away more, adding further to pollution.

Since the 1980s, the high-tech boom has produced a new type of pollution from discarded electronic and electrical equipment such as computers, televisions, game consoles and mobile phones. These can release toxic chemicals such as lead, mercury and cadmium into the environment.

A different way of thinking

Why are we creating so much pollution? When we make, use and dispose of things, we think in straight lines. We start by extracting resources. We then produce objects, distribute them, consume them, and finally dump what is not needed anymore. We do not think about the pollution created at each step of the process. By contrast, the earth's natural systems, like the water cycle, run in circles. In nature, there is no such thing as waste or pollution. Everything is constantly being recycled. Waste from one animal is food for another.

Developments in science and technology have led to enormous improvements in our lives, but we have failed to take account of the cost of these improvements. We buy products only to dump them soon after, responding to the latest fashion or trend. It is often cheaper to buy a new television than have it repaired. Many products we buy, such as plastic cups, cameras and batteries, are designed to be used only briefly before being thrown away. They are often made of artificial materials that do not decompose easily or quickly. Instead, they build up in the environment and affect the quality of the air we breathe, the water we drink and the soil we grow food in.

DEBATE

You are in charge

You are representing your school in a regional youth forum to discuss the problem of pollution in your area. Which proposals do you think will best address the problem?

- Find out what the main sources of pollution are in your area and stage protests against the polluters.
- Force the factories or people responsible for polluting the environment to pay for the clean up by giving them fines.
- Push the government to set stricter standards for pollution.
- Provide information on air, water and ground pollution levels in your locality and send out letters to local residents informing them of problems in their area.

CHAPTER 2

The Air We Breathe

It is 2025. Maria's family lives in an apartment in Los Angeles. Today, the meteorological office has announced another 'code red' day and, as a safety measure, Maria's school is closed. It used to be fun to miss school, but this is happening more often as the weather is changing. Walking to school and outdoor sports are not advisable on hot days when brown smoke hangs over the city. The air is heavy with fumes from factories, waste incinerators, cars and lorries. Next year, Maria is joining a virtual school so she can learn from home through internet-based tutoring.

Our unique atmosphere

The atmosphere is a thin blanket of gases that surrounds the earth. It is essential for the survival of life on the planet. The atmosphere moves heat and water around the globe and protects living things from the sun's harmful radiation. Our atmosphere has just the right balance of chemicals to sustain life. These move around continuously between sky, ocean, soil, plants and animals. For example, trees absorb carbon dioxide from the air and produce oxygen. When trees die, carbon is released back into the atmosphere.

A very thin layer around the earth, called the troposphere, is the only part of the atmosphere in which living things can breathe. About 78 per cent of the air we breathe is made of nitrogen, and 21 per cent is oxygen. The rest is made of other gases such as water vapour and carbon dioxide.

Kaohsiung in Taiwan, like many industrial cities, suffers from air pollution. People often wear face masks to protect themselves from the fumes.

Before the expansion of cities and the development of industry, the earth's own natural systems kept the air fairly clean. Wind dispersed fumes and rain washed dust into the ground, rivers and seas. Since the Industrial Revolution, humans have started to upset the delicate balance of the atmosphere by releasing more pollutants than nature can diffuse. Air pollution has become a global problem.

What is air pollution?

Air pollution is gases, dust and fumes in the air that can harm people, animals and plants. These gases, dust and fumes are called pollutants. Some pollutants are visible, like smoke from car exhausts, and dust. Others are invisible, like emissions from cattle or chemicals released by factories. Some of these pollutants are the result of natural disasters such as forest fires and erupting volcanoes. However, most air pollution comes from a single human activity: the burning of fossil fuels to power cars and factories and to produce electricity.

MAIN SOURCES OF AIR POLLUTION

Substance	Combustion of fuel in cars and other vehicles	Burning of fossil fuels to power factories	Burning of fossil fuels to produce energy in power stations	Disposal of waste in landfill sites	Burning of waste in incinerators	Emissions from intensive cattle farming
Carbon dioxide	✖	✖	✖			
Carbon monoxide	✖	✖	✖		✖	
Sulphur dioxide		✖	✖			
Nitrogen oxides	✖	✖	✖			
Particulates	✖	✖	✖		✖	
Methane		✖	✖	✖		✖
Heavy metals (e.g. lead, mercury and cadmium)	✖	✖	✖	✖	✖	

Source: Data compiled from UK Air Quality Archive; UK Department for Environment, Food and Rural Affairs; Environment Agency

Transport

Cars are a major source of air pollution. Car engines burn a mixture of air and petrol vapour. This releases tiny particles and chemicals into the atmosphere. The main ones are carbon monoxide, carbon dioxide and nitrogen oxides. Breathing these toxic gases and tiny particles can cause lung and heart diseases.

Some of these gases change into other gases once in the air, because of chemical reactions. These other gases are called secondary pollutants. For example, waste gases from cars react with sunlight to form a gas called ozone. The effect is smog. This is different from the smog in cities hundreds of years ago (see pages 8–9). It is photochemical smog – a brownish haze that floats over cities, most often on warm, sunny days. Los Angeles and Mexico City are badly affected by smog.

Other sources of air pollution

Power stations are another major source of air pollution. When we burn fossil fuels to generate power for homes, offices and factories, we release carbon dioxide and other harmful gases.

Factories also contribute to air pollution. Each industry produces a different type of air pollution. Metal production is the main industrial source of air pollution, releasing sulphur dioxide and highly toxic heavy metals. Exposure to these chemicals can affect people's health in many ways. Steel factories, paper mills, chemical and cement plants all produce massive quantities of toxic fine particles.

Intensive farming is another cause of air pollution. The spraying of fertilizers to enrich the soil and pesticides to kill insects releases harmful chemicals such as nitrous oxide into the air. Large amounts of manure from cattle farming produce toxic gases such as ammonia. The digestive gases emitted by cattle pollute the air with methane.

Santiago, capital of Chile, is badly affected by smog. The city lies in a valley, bordered by the Andes mountains. Pollutants from cars and factories get trapped over the city for days.

Methane traps heat in the atmosphere and contributes to global warming (see pages 16–17).

Finally, the way we dispose of our waste causes air pollution. Burning waste releases dangerous chemicals such as dioxins and heavy metals and produces toxic ashes. Burying waste in landfills produces harmful substances such as methane and lead.

The carbon cycle

Why does burning fossil fuels produce pollution? Looking at the carbon cycle helps us understand. All living things contain carbon. Carbon is also in the oceans, air and rocks. In the atmosphere, carbon is attached to oxygen in a gas called carbon dioxide. Plants absorb carbon dioxide and sunlight to make their own food, and they release oxygen. This is called photosynthesis. The carbon becomes part of the plant. Animals take in carbon when they eat plants and other animals.

This diagram shows the natural processes that move carbon around the earth. Carbon atoms are constantly being exchanged – between one living thing and another and between living things and the environment. However, the total amount of carbon on earth always remains the same.

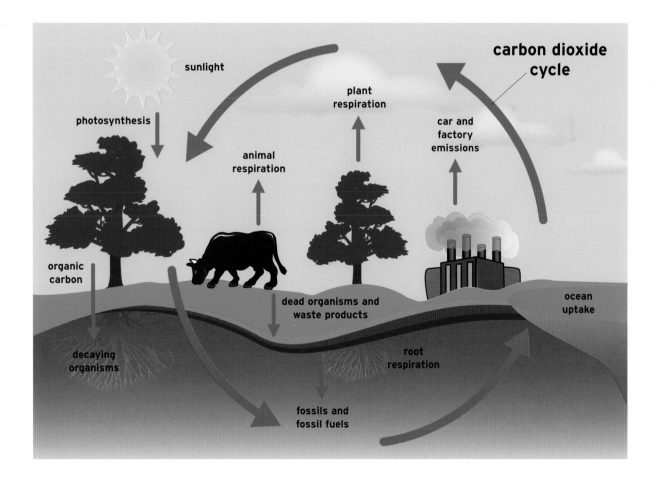

sunlight

plant respiration

carbon dioxide cycle

photosynthesis

car and factory emissions

animal respiration

organic carbon

dead organisms and waste products

ocean uptake

decaying organisms

root respiration

fossils and fossil fuels

Carbon dioxide is released back into the atmosphere when animals breathe out and when their remains decompose in the soil. Fossil fuels such as coal, oil and natural gas come from the remains of plants and tiny marine animals buried in the soil and compressed by heat and pressure over time. Fossil fuels take millions of years to form. When we burn fossil fuels to produce energy, this carbon is unlocked and released back into the air as carbon dioxide.

Today we are releasing much more carbon dioxide into the air than the earth's plants and oceans can naturally absorb. We are also cutting down large areas of forest, so there are fewer trees to absorb carbon.

Global warming

Most scientists believe that the burning of fossil fuels is starting to affect the earth's climate. The earth is getting warmer. This is causing the water of the oceans to expand, polar ice caps to melt and sea levels to rise.

Polar bears could be extinct within 20 years because of global warming. As the Arctic sea ice melts, they are forced to swim further in their hunt for seals.

To understand how this is happening, it helps to think of our atmosphere as a kind of greenhouse. When sunlight heats the earth's surface, some of it is reflected back into space. However, much of the heat gets trapped in the atmosphere by natural gases such as water vapour, carbon dioxide and methane. They are like the glass walls of a greenhouse, keeping the earth warm. Without these natural 'greenhouse gases', heat would escape back into space and the earth would be too cold to sustain life.

The problem is that since we began burning fossil fuels on a large scale during the Industrial Revolution, too much heat from the sun is getting trapped in the atmosphere. As a result, the earth is growing warmer.

Burning fossil fuels releases carbon dioxide, which accounts for 80 per cent of human-made greenhouse gases. Another important greenhouse gas is methane. It is produced from the decay of rubbish in landfills and the extraction of coal and natural gas. Scientists estimate that the digestive gases emitted by cattle produce between 15 and 20 per cent of global methane emissions.

This chart shows the proportion of global greenhouse gas emissions created by different areas of human activity.

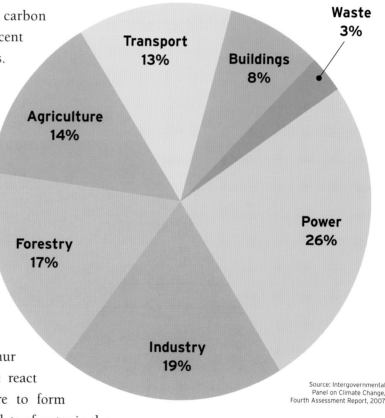

Source: Intergovernmental Panel on Climate Change, Fourth Assessment Report, 2007

Acid rain

When we burn fossil fuels in power stations, factories, houses and cars, we produce toxic gases such as sulphur dioxide and nitrogen oxides. These react with other gases in the atmosphere to form strong acids. They mix with tiny droplets of water in the air and get carried by strong winds over long distances before they fall back on earth as acid rain, snow or hail. The acid rain in Scandinavia is caused by emissions from the United Kingdom and other northern European countries. Acid rain damages trees and plants and makes lakes and rivers more acidic, harming fish and other wildlife.

Holes in the ozone layer

About 15 to 30 kilometres above the earth is a layer of our atmosphere that contains high concentrations of a gas called ozone, which is a form of oxygen. The ozone layer absorbs the sun's harmful ultraviolet rays, preventing most of them from reaching the earth. These rays cause your skin to tan, but too much exposure to them can cause skin cancer. Life on earth could not survive without the protective shield of the ozone layer.

Each spring, a hole as big as the United States forms in the ozone layer over the South Pole. A smaller hole develops over the North Pole. The holes have been caused by a group of polluting gases known as CFCs (short for chlorofluorocarbons). CFCs were first produced in the 1930s and were used in spray cans, refrigerators, air conditioning systems and fire extinguishers.

Scientists discovered that, high in the atmosphere, chlorine atoms escape from CFCs, destroying ozone. In 1996, most industrialized countries banned the use of CFCs, but these gases will stay in the

This photo shows victims of one of the world's worst industrial disasters, in Bhopal, India, in December 1984. Toxic gas leaked from the Union Carbide pesticide factory and floated over the crowded city of Bhopal. Thousands of people died instantly and many more were injured.

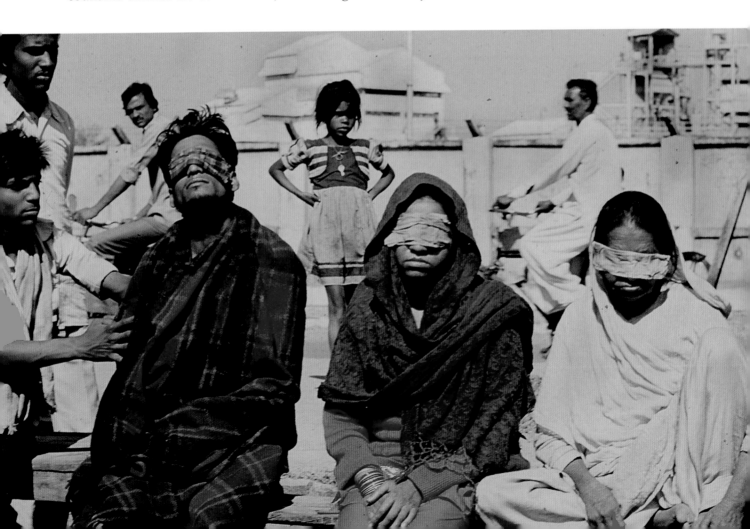

atmosphere for a long time. They are also released when we throw old fridges and air conditioning equipment onto landfills.

Dangerous leaks

Accidents in chemical factories and nuclear power plants can cause large-scale air pollution with often devastating effects on people and the environment. One of the biggest disasters of this kind occurred when a leak of toxic gases from the Union Carbide pesticide factory drifted over the Indian city of Bhopal in 1984. Between 15,000 and 20,000 people died and up to 200,000 were injured.

Accidents at nuclear power plants can cause the release of high levels of radiation. People who are exposed to too much radiation can suffer tissue damage and diseases such as cancer. The world's worst nuclear accident occurred in 1986 at the Chernobyl nuclear power plant in Ukraine. A reactor exploded and sent a radioactive cloud over much of Western Europe. More than 56 people were killed instantly but the health of thousands more was affected. Instances of cancer and birth defects rose dramatically in the surrounding area.

DEBATE

You are in charge

You are taking part in a debate on how to deal with global warming. Which of the following statements do you support?

- Global warming is not caused by human activity. It is a natural phenomenon, and we should not worry about it.
- We can reduce air pollution through new technologies such as greener cars or capturing carbon emissions from factories.
- We can reduce air pollution by using nuclear power, as it does not involve burning fossil fuels.
- We can reduce air pollution by using renewable sources of energy, such as wind and solar power.
- We can reduce air pollution by reducing our energy use.

Every Drop Counts

It is 2025. An old woman is sitting with her granddaughter by the River Ganges in Kolkata, India. 'When I was young,' she says, 'this was a sacred river where we used to scatter the ashes of our loved ones according to Hindu tradition. The river was pure and at times you would see garlands of flowers floating to remember the dead. The river was alive and fishermen came here to find food. Today, the river is smelly and lifeless. It has become the city's dump. Every day, raw sewage is pumped into the river. Factories pour out their dirty water. This is why we are short of water. This is why we are at war with other countries fighting over water sources, because we have destroyed our own.'

Water cycle

Isn't it amazing that the water you drink has been recycled over and over for more than 3.5 billion years? Since the formation of the earth, the same water has been continuously on the move. The sun's heat causes water in rivers, lakes and seas to evaporate. The water vapour cools as it rises and turns back into tiny water droplets to form clouds.

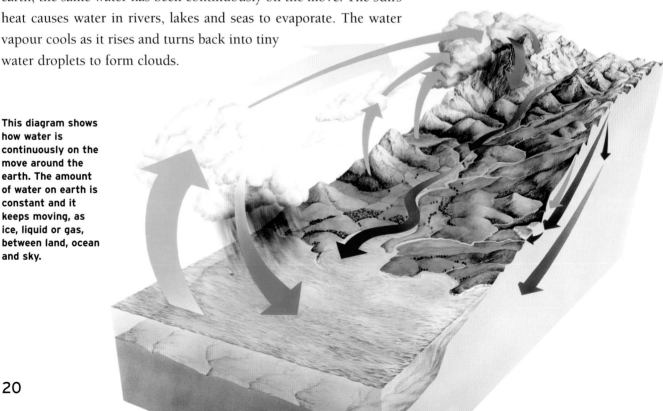

This diagram shows how water is continuously on the move around the earth. The amount of water on earth is constant and it keeps moving, as ice, liquid or gas, between land, ocean and sky.

When the clouds become too heavy, water falls back to earth as rain, hail or snow.

Some falls directly back into lakes and oceans. Some collects into rivers and streams before returning to larger bodies of water, where it evaporates again. Some soaks slowly into the ground to become part of the groundwater, a huge reservoir of freshwater for plants and animals. Plants release water back into the atmosphere through a process called transpiration. And the cycle goes on and on.

As the world population continues to grow and industry expands, we are putting increasing pressure on the limited amount of water on our planet. By pumping polluting gases into the air, spraying chemicals on the soil to grow food and dumping waste into rivers and seas, we are affecting our water.

What is water pollution?

Water pollution occurs when unwanted substances end up in rivers, lakes, seas and groundwater, harming plants, animals and people. Water can be polluted deliberately, by the dumping of harmful substances, such as sewage or factory waste, into water sources. To reduce this type of pollution, most industrialized countries have adopted strict laws.

Water can also be polluted unintentionally, by substances produced far away that are transported by rain, rivers and ocean currents. As rain flows over the ground, it picks up and carries toxic substances from farms, industrial sites, mines, building sites, gardens, roads and rubbish dumps. These end up in streams, rivers, lakes and oceans. They also soak into the soil, affecting the groundwater.

Top: Freshwater makes up a very small fraction of the earth's total water supply.
Bottom: This diagram shows the sources of the earth's freshwater. Most freshwater is stored in ice caps and glaciers.

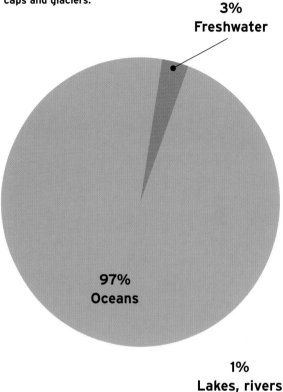

3%
Freshwater

97%
Oceans

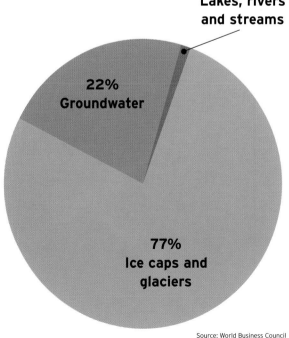

1%
Lakes, rivers and streams

22%
Groundwater

77%
Ice caps and glaciers

Source: World Business Council for Sustainable Development

Ocean currents move massive amounts of water and pollutants around the globe. In 1992, a cargo ship travelling from Hong Kong to the United States hit a storm in the Pacific Ocean. Many containers were washed overboard, including one with thousands of bath toys. Since then these plastic ducks have been found all over the world from Hawaii to Iceland and the North Pole. Water pollution does not recognize national borders. It is a global problem.

(opposite) Nearly all the major rivers in the world are affected by industrial pollution. The pulp and paper industry is a major source of pollution. Here, waste water from a paper mill is being discharged straight into the Qingai river in China.

Pollution from industry

Nearly all the lakes, rivers and oceans of the world contain some level of industrial pollution. Factories use large amounts of water to make, wash and dilute products. After the water is used, it is put back into rivers, along with any toxic waste produced in the process. Governments in many countries have adopted laws to ensure that waste water is cleaned before being released. Despite this, factories in many parts of the world continue to dump industrial waste into rivers and seas. This industrial waste contains toxic substances such as lead, asbestos and mercury. Many of these substances do not break down naturally over time. Instead, they build up in the environment and can be harmful to plants and animals.

One such substance is mercury. Mercury can damage the nervous and reproductive systems of mammals, including humans. Mercury is emitted mainly by coal-fired power plants, but also by smelting and cement production. When mercury waste ends up in the sea, it is absorbed by tiny creatures called phytoplankton. When the phytoplankton are eaten by small fish, the mercury stays in the fish. The small fish are in turn eaten by larger fish, such as tuna, which then become food for people and animals. The result is that large amounts of mercury end up in animals at the top of the food chain. This is called bioaccumulation.

THE TIME IT TAKES FOR DIFFERENT ITEMS TO DEGRADE IN WATER

Cardboard	2 weeks
Newspaper	6 weeks
Foam	50 years
Styrofoam	80 years
Aluminium	200 years
Plastic	Between 1,000 years and forever
Glass	It takes so long that we don't know the exact time

Source: www.water-pollution.org.uk/marine.html

Pollution from sewage

Sewage is a major source of water pollution. It is biodegradable, so in small amounts it can break down naturally in the soil. However, the human population of six and a half billion produces a huge amount of sewage, and the earth cannot absorb this naturally. The problem is made worse by the vast quantity of artificial substances we flush down our drains. These are not biodegradable. Every day we use shampoos, soap, toothpaste, detergents, hair dyes and cleaning products. Many of these contain synthetic (artificial) chemicals. Have you ever thought about where all this goes?

In industrialized countries, most sewage is carried away from homes through a network of pipes and ends up in treatment plants. Here the sewage is cleaned by chemicals and bacteria, which eat germs and dirt. The cleaned water is pumped back into the nearest river. In some countries, the sludge (solid leftovers) is dumped in landfill sites or burned in incinerators. In others it is turned into fertilizers to enrich the soil. However, some toxic substances remain in the water, even after treatment.

In many developing countries, most sewage is discharged directly into rivers and streams without any treatment. About 40 per cent of the world's population live in areas where there is no collection of sewage and no treatment facilities. Many people do not have access to safe drinking water. Each year over five million people die from diseases such as cholera, diarrhoea and typhoid, caused by drinking water polluted by sewage.

In many countries, raw sewage is pumped directly into the sea with little or no treatment. As it contains high levels of nitrogen, ammonia and other contaminants, it can create serious problems for marine life and swimmers.

Pollution from agriculture

Since the beginning of the 20th century, farmers have adopted intensive farming techniques in order to boost their yields and satisfy the demand of the world's growing population. Today, intensive farming relies on the use of herbicides, pesticides and fertilizers. These are sprayed on fields to kill weeds and insects or to boost the growth of food crops. They contain toxic chemicals such as nitrogen and phosphorus. When it rains, these chemicals are washed through the soil and end up in nearby rivers and lakes. Medications and hormones used by farmers to make animals grow larger and more quickly also often end up in the water supply.

Chemical fertilizers and manure from farm animals contain nutrients such as nitrates and phosphates. Sometimes these fertilizers run off into nearby rivers and lakes, causing an increase in nutrients. Too many nutrients in the water cause plants and algae to grow very fast. The water becomes cloudy and green. This is called algal bloom. The algae may absorb all the oxygen in the water, leaving none for other plants and fish. They also block sunlight for plants living under the water surface. About half the lakes in Asia, Europe and North and South America are polluted by nutrients.

MAIN SOURCES OF WATER POLLUTION

Pollutant	Industrial waste	Waste from cars carried by wind, rain and run-off water	Sewage	Agricultural waste	Mining waste	Household waste	Waste from landfills leaching into the ground
Organic matter (waste from plants and animals)	✖		✖	✖			✖
Nutrients	✖		✖	✖			
Heavy metals	✖	✖			✖		✖
Oil	✖	✖	✖	✖		✖	✖
Toxic chemicals	✖	✖	✖	✖	✖	✖	✖

Source: www.earthtrends.org

Oil and water do not mix

Major oil tanker spills often make the headlines as they can have devastating effects on the marine environment. One of the worst oil spills occurred when the *Exxon Valdez* sank off the coast of Alaska in 1989. The tanker ran aground on rocks and spilled 40 million litres of crude oil into the sea. The oil eventually covered 28,000 square kilometres of ocean, more than 22,000 times the surface of an Olympic swimming pool. Thousands of fish, ducks, sea otters, seals and seabirds died.

Oil cannot dissolve in water and forms a thick sludge. It suffocates fish, gets caught in the feathers of marine birds and blocks light for aquatic plants. It also affects people whose livelihood depends on fishing and tourism in coastal areas.

In January 2000, the oil tanker *Al Jazya 1* sank off the coast of the United Arab Emirates in bad weather. It spilt 200 to 300 tonnes of oil and caused a 900-metre-long oil slick.

However, accidental spills from oil tankers only make up about 12 per cent of the oil that enters the sea. The rest comes from ships flushing their tanks out at sea, oil platforms and motorboats. Large volumes of oil are also poured down the drain or carried into the sea by rain. Rainwater picks up drips of oil from cars, petrol stations, tractors, leaky storage tanks and industrial machinery.

Plastic pollution

Plastic is the most common material used to make things today. It is popular because it is light, durable and cheap to produce. It can also be easily moulded into different shapes. Also, plastic does not break down easily. Its molecules are very large and tightly bonded together and so resist decomposition. For these reasons, plastic makes up a very large proportion of today's pollution. It is estimated that of all the rubbish floating in the oceans, 90 per cent is plastic. If you go to a beach anywhere in the world, you are likely to see plastic litter washed up by the waves.

Plastic pollution can harm seabirds, fish and other marine animals. According to conservation groups, millions of seabirds and 100,000 mammals and sea turtles die each year by getting entangled in fishing lines and nets or by swallowing tiny pieces of plastic. About 80 per cent of plastic pollution comes from items that have been thrown away on land and are then carried out to sea by rivers, wind and tide. The rest comes from private and commercial ships, oil platforms and spilled containers from cargo ships.

Scientists have recently discovered a huge area of plastic waste twice the size of Texas, floating in the northern Pacific Ocean. A slow, swirling current traps plastic debris from all over the world. They named it the Great Pacific Garbage Patch and predict that it will double in the next ten years.

DEBATE

You are in charge

A 20-year-old oil tanker strikes rocks in a storm. The tanker is leaking oil. The ship is carrying 400,000 tons of crude oil. Who is responsible?

- The oil company that hired the ship to transport oil to the refinery?
- The ship's captain, who is in charge of what happens to the vessel?
- Consumers, who demand oil for their energy needs?
- Governments, for failing to pass laws to prevent old and unsafe vessels from being used on the world's oceans?

What can be done to avoid such a disaster in the future?

Soaking into the Soil

It is 2025. Four years ago, the Jones family bought the house of their dreams. It is on an estate in the centre of town, so the family can walk or cycle to school, to work and to the local shops. Yet the house is in a quiet location and has a big garden. Last year, the whole family started to develop breathing problems, allergies and skin rashes. Their neighbours also began to suffer similar health problems. The local community discovered that at the beginning of the century, dangerous waste had been buried underground in containers around 20 kilometres away. Scientists reassured the population that these hi-tech containers were safe and could not leak toxic pollution into the soil. But the Joneses and their neighbours are not sure they believe them.

What is land pollution?

Land pollution occurs when unwanted substances end up on the land or in the ground. The main cause of land pollution is the production and disposal of consumer goods and intensive farming. To make things in factories, we extract tonnes of raw materials, such as metals, sand and crude oil, leaving heaps of mining waste behind. This waste often contains toxic substances that will contaminate the soil.

As the world population rises, so production must increase to keep pace with demand, and the amount of rubbish we throw away becomes ever greater. We are also creating more synthetic substances that do not decompose naturally and, instead, accumulate in the environment.

The demand for food is also increasing, so we farm the land more intensively, spraying chemicals to boost productivity and to get rid of weeds and insects. These chemicals slowly soak into the ground.

NEW CHEMICALS FOR INDUSTRY

Up to 100,000 synthetic chemicals are used by industry today and over 700 new ones are added each year. Very few chemicals have been tested for their effects on plants and animals.

Source: www.storyofstuff.com

We dispose of flammable, explosive or poisonous waste by burying it in underground containers, which sometimes leak into the soil.

A chemical world

In 1962 Rachel Carson, an American biologist, wrote a famous book called *Silent Spring*. In this book she describes the danger of using strong chemicals such as dichlorodiphenyltrichloroethane (DDT). This is one of the most powerful pesticides ever produced and can kill hundreds of different kinds of insects at once. Carson explained how chemicals like DDT accumulate in the food chain and end up poisoning birds and animals. Her book launched the global environmental movement and led to a worldwide ban of DDT. However, since then, many other chemicals have been developed. These are used all over the world to make food, clothes, furniture, electric appliances and cars. When these products are disposed of, many of the toxic substances used to make them remain in the environment, polluting soil, air and water.

A plane sprays pesticide on carrot crops in the Rio Grande Valley in Texas, USA. The use of toxic chemicals for intensive farming is a major source of soil pollution and many people campaign to ban their use.

The journey of a mobile phone

For each product we make, we produce a huge amount of pollution, both at the start and the end of its life. Have you ever thought about the pollution created just by a mobile phone? The world has more than three billion mobile phones. Nearly half of them are made in China, but the raw materials come from all over the world. Each phone contains about 400 different parts. These include handsets, circuit boards, keypads and batteries.

A large percentage of the pollution caused by making mobile phones comes from the extraction of raw materials. The circuit board is made from copper, gold, lead, nickel, zinc, beryllium, tantalum, coltan, and other metals. Batteries contain nickel, cobalt, zinc, cadmium, and copper. To obtain these materials, raw materials need to be mined around the world and refined in factories. Mining involves clearing forests, digging pits and using chemicals to extract ore from rock, leaving behind tonnes of toxic mud. Fossil fuels are burned to transport raw materials and to assemble the mobile phones in factories.

There are more than three billion mobile phones currently in circulation around the world. These phones are constantly being discarded, releasing their toxic components into the environment.

Valuable natural resources, such as trees (for paper), crude oil (for plastic), aluminium and other materials are used to package the phones once they are made. The phones are then transported to their destinations around the world, consuming yet more fossil fuels (and creating yet more pollution) in the process.

Most mobile phones are thrown away after two years and end up buried in landfill sites. All the valuable gold, silver, copper and other resources inside them can never be retrieved. Some of the substances inside mobile phones, known as 'persistent toxins', can stay in the environment for long periods of time, even after disposal. They can leach into the ground and find their way into our water.

What about recycling? Many schemes involve sending old phones to China, Pakistan and India, where people dismantle them by hand to recover the valuable materials. The leftovers are often dumped in fields, ponds and rivers, polluting the land and water of other countries. And this is the story of just one product, the mobile phone!

Here are some of the parts of a mobile phone. Dismantling old phones for recycling is slow and expensive as it has to be done manually. Researchers are looking at more efficient ways of recovering valuable materials and disposing of toxic mobile phone parts.

COMPUTERS

Over a billion computers are in use worldwide. In 2007, about 268 million computers were sold. Sixty-seven million of them were bought in the United States. It is predicted that 426 million computers will be sold worldwide in 2012. The manufacture of a new computer and monitor uses up 240 grammes of fossil fuels, 22 kilogrammes of chemicals and 1,500 litres of water. A PC is typically 40 per cent steel, 30-40 per cent plastic, 10 per cent aluminium and 10 per cent other metals, including copper, gold, silver, cadmium and platinum.

Source: www.e-takeback.org

Landfills and incinerators

What happens to all the industrial and domestic waste we produce?
In many countries, the rubbish is collected and taken to landfills,
where it is carefully buried in the ground. Landfills cause pollution.
As paper, food and other waste break down, large amounts of
methane and carbon dioxide are released, contributing to global
warming. Pollution from old landfills can slowly leak into the
ground over time and affect the water we drink. Also, as old landfills
get full, we are running out of space for new sites.

In many developing countries,
people make a living by
recovering valuable materials
from rubbish dumps. About 15
families live in houses made
from recycled waste in the Al-
Taqi rubbish dump in northern
Baghdad, Iraq. They sift
through the waste for glass,
plastic or any other valuable
material that they can sell.

In other countries, most rubbish is burned in incinerators. This method of disposal takes less space than landfills and many people think it is safer. However, burning waste produces toxic ash, which needs to be buried somewhere. Some materials, such as plastics and textiles, release toxic gases in the air.

In many poor countries, millions of people living on the edge of expanding cities do not have any waste collection. They are forced to dump their rubbish in streets, rivers and ditches. However, in other ways poorer countries set a good example to wealthier nations. With limited resources, repair and reuse is often common practice. Wood, metal and plastic waste can find a new life as building material for homes. Empty cans are turned into water containers or children's toys. Old tyres are made into sandals, and flammable materials are a source of fuel.

Nuclear waste

To reduce our dependence on fossil fuels, many countries are opting for a different source of energy, nuclear power. Unlike fossil fuels, nuclear power produces very few emissions of polluting gases. However, it does produce highly toxic waste, which can take more than 20,000 years to become harmless. Nuclear waste is radioactive – it gives off invisible energy rays that can seriously harm people's health. Nuclear waste is currently buried in specially designed containers, but scientists are looking at better ways of getting rid of such dangerous waste. One possibility being explored by the United States is the long-term storage of high-level radioactive waste deep below the earth's surface. Many people are opposed to this option as no one can guarantee that waste will not leak.

DEBATE

You are in charge
You are thrilled to get a new mobile phone for your birthday. What do you do with your old mobile phone?

- Give it to a family member or a charity shop.
- Send it back to the company that made it because they have a policy of recycling and reusing components.
- Send it to a company that refits old phones.
- Throw it out. It's so small it's not going to be a big problem in a landfill.

Think about a day in your life and all the things you buy, consume and throw away.
What three things could you do to help reduce the amount of waste you send to landfills or incinerators?

A Different Way

It is 2025 and Zara and her family have moved to their eco-home. The facades of the house capture energy from the sun. Grass grows on the roof to keep the house cool in summer and warm in winter. Gas produced from sewage is used for cooking. A small wind turbine fitted on the chimney generates much of their electricity. Rainwater filtered by plants is collected for activities such as washing clothes and watering the vegetable patch. The family cycle or walk when they can and own a car powered by hydrogen. They compost their food waste and try to repair and recycle as much as they can.

We cannot go on like this

The earth is polluted because of the way we make and dispose of things, power our vehicles and use energy in our homes. We dig out natural resources to supply our factories and power stations, leaving behind large amounts of toxic waste. We burn huge amounts of fossil fuels to produce energy, releasing toxic gases into the air. Pollutants in the air mix with rain, affecting rivers, lakes and oceans. Waste from factories and power stations is discharged straight into rivers and seas. Products are designed to have a short lifespan, so we produce mountains of rubbish. We bury valuable materials in landfills all over the world and burn toxic products. Some of the substances we

A campaigner from the environmental pressure group Greenpeace, dressed as a polar bear, hugs the earth at the opening ceremony of the 2007 United Nations conference on climate change in Bali.

produce are so dangerous that they will have to be carefully monitored for thousands of years to come. This is not sustainable. We cannot carry on like this forever.

What is being done?

Pollution ignores borders. A polluted river flows across countries, and global warming affects everyone in the world. As a global problem, pollution needs a global solution. In recent decades some progress has been made. Political and business leaders have negotiated international agreements and passed laws to reduce pollution.

World leaders adopted the Montreal Protocol in 1987 to ban the production of chemicals damaging the ozone layer. The Basel Convention, agreed in 1989, controlled the movement of dangerous waste from one country to another. In 1992, an Earth Summit was held in Rio de Janeiro, Brazil, where 179 world leaders met to discuss environmental issues. They produced a document called Agenda 21, which stressed the need to do more with less resources and to adopt cleaner technology. Agenda 21 promoted the 'polluters pay' principle by which polluters are responsible for the waste they create.

MAIN INTERNATIONAL AGREEMENTS ON POLLUTION

Date adopted	Name of agreement	Purpose
1972	London Dumping Convention	To regulate what can and cannot be dumped into the sea
1987	The Montreal Protocol	To protect the ozone layer by taking action to control global emissions of CFCs
1989	Basel Convention	To control the movement of hazardous waste from one country to another
1992	Climate Change Convention	To stabilize greenhouse gas emissions and encourage scientific research into climate change
1997	Kyoto Protocol	To tackle climate change and reduce carbon dioxide emissions

In 1997, an important agreement was adopted at an international conference in Kyoto, Japan, to cut the amount of gases that industries produce. The Kyoto Protocol came into force in 2005. Two years later, further targets to reduce emissions were discussed at another summit in Bali, Indonesia.

Although these agreements have helped to reduce pollution, the problem is that many of them are voluntary. Governments who sign them do not have to act upon them. Even when these agreements become law, there is no real penalty for governments who do not conform. Sometimes the biggest polluters do not join these agreements. For example, the United States is one of the world's largest emitters of carbon dioxide, but it has not ratified (given formal approval to) the Kyoto Protocol.

Learning from nature

Some people believe that the best way to tackle pollution is to use technologies and systems that imitate the natural world. Nature uses resources efficiently. Everything is interconnected and materials are used and reused over and over again. Our current approach is to take natural resources from the earth and to transform them into materials that cannot be returned safely into the environment.

A different way of designing and making things would be to use resources more efficiently and to think of waste as a resource in its

TERMITE VENTILATION

Termite mounds were the inspiration for a new kind of ventilation system. Termites build their mounds in a certain way to maintain the temperature inside their nest despite varying conditions outside. Ventilation holes at the bottom of the mound allow fresh air to enter, while hot, stale air is forced out of the top. Termites open and close these holes to adjust the temperature as needed. Buildings fitted with a similar ventilation system use up to 90 per cent less energy for air conditioning than conventional buildings of the same size.

own right. Products that are no longer needed can be composted and turned into food for plants and animals. Or they could be used as materials for new products.

Nature has many examples of materials and processes that we can copy. For example, we can learn to design new buildings by looking at trees. The surface of the building can capture sunlight to produce energy through solar panels. Rain can be collected and filtered naturally by plants. It can then be used for activities that do not require pure water, such as flushing the toilet. We could even use a mechanism similar to a tree's roots to draw water from the ground.

In 2007, the Trott family built their new eco-home in Normandy, France. Their house is made entirely from recycled and natural materials, such as old tyres, aluminium cans and bottles. They use renewable energy from the sun and wind and harvest water from rain and snow. All waste is treated on site.

Nature was also the model for a new kind of outdoor paint, developed in Germany, that resists dirt and mould. The paint's inventors were inspired by the white lotus, which always has immaculately clean leaves. The leaves are covered with microscopic needles. Dust or dirt falling on the leaves gets stuck on the needles. When a raindrop rolls across the needles, it picks up the dirt and carries it away. The paint uses a similar principle to keep itself clean, reducing the need for pollution-creating detergents.

A better understanding of natural processes can allow us to maintain a comfortable lifestyle without damaging the planet.

Clean production

Instead of spending time and money cleaning up pollution, why not use methods that do not pollute in the first place? Today, many

In many countries, waste is a valuable resource. Here, toy vehicles made from recycled tins and aerosol cans are on display at a market in Antananarivo, Madagascar.

governments and businesses are investing in cleaner technologies that will help conserve resources and reduce pollution. These technologies include electric cars, capture of carbon emissions from power stations and solar energy.

This approach means thinking in cycles, as nature does, rather than in straight lines. For example, leather trainers can now be produced without any toxic products, so they can be composted at the end of their life. Books can be made of plastic and washable vegetable ink. When they are no longer needed, the ink can be washed off and they can be reprinted as a different book. Think of all the trees this would save.

Other businesses are looking into leasing products to customers rather than selling them. They are also looking at designing products to be taken apart and reassembled, so they never need to be thrown away. For example, a mobile phone could be leased to a customer for a number of years, then taken back when it is broken or needs upgrading. Instead of sending the old phone to a landfill, valuable parts could be taken out and reused in a new one. The other parts could be recycled. As the famous physicist Albert Einstein said, if we want to solve problems, we need to think in a different way from the way we were thinking when we created the problem.

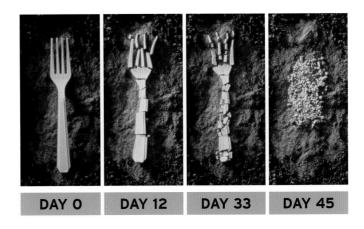

| DAY 0 | DAY 12 | DAY 33 | DAY 45 |

This fork, made out of a new kind of corn-based plastic, decomposes in just 45 days.

DEBATE

You are in charge

You are an architect. A client has asked you to design a house of the future that mimics nature and reduces pollution.

- What materials would you use to build it?

- How would you design it in terms of shape, size and general layout?

- What sources of energy would you use to provide heat and electricity?

- How would you insulate it from the elements?

- What would you do to make sure the homeowner could minimize waste, and reuse and recycle as much as possible?

Things You Can Do

It is 2025. An international youth summit on pollution is being held in Beijing, China. Young people feel betrayed by the way their parents and previous generations have damaged the environment. More than half of the world population is under 25 years old and they feel they are not being heard on issues that affect their lives. Working with the United Nations, a group of young people will represent their countries and help identify priorities for the next decade.

Over to us

Every time we use a computer, watch television or cook a meal, we burn fossil fuels and pollute the atmosphere. Every time we throw old clothes, CDs or plastic bags in the bin, we add to the mountain of rubbish produced every day. When we pour paint, oil and other toxic substances down the drain or into rivers, we pollute the water we drink. By changing the way we consume goods, we can make a huge difference. Our own actions, combined with the actions of millions of others, can help to reduce pollution.

Using less energy

A great deal of pollution is created by the energy we use to heat and light our homes, power our cars and fly abroad. About 85 per cent of the energy used in the world comes from burning fossil fuels, which releases carbon dioxide and other harmful gases. So a good way of reducing pollution is to use less energy at home, at school and everywhere we go. If it gets cold, instead of turning up the heat, just put on an extra jumper. The worst energy guzzlers in your house are tumble dryers, computers and lighting. So it makes sense to switch off lights, turn off your computer when you are not using it and unplug appliances with standby buttons.

You can take action by trying to use less energy at home. A good way of reducing pollution is to switch off lights and tell the rest of your family to do the same.

Another way to save electricity is to use energy-efficient light bulbs. They use 75 per cent less energy and last ten times longer than conventional bulbs. One downside to these bulbs is that they contain mercury, which can escape if the glass is broken. Make sure you dispose of old bulbs safely.

Also, why not use the sun to dry your clothes, power your calculator or recharge your MP3 player? Talk to your family about the possibility of switching over to renewable energy, such as solar power. Also, you can save energy by eating fruit and vegetables in season. Growing strawberries in greenhouses in the winter, for example, uses up a great deal of electricity.

Solar power is an increasingly important energy source in many countries. Solar panels convert sunlight into electricity and can be used to provide heat and hot water for homes.

A TYPICAL SUNDAY ROAST

A study looking at a typical Sunday lunch near Leicester, England, found that the beef had travelled 21,462 kilometres from Australia, the potatoes 2,447 kilometres from Italy, the carrots 9,620 kilometres from South Africa and the beans 9,532 kilometres from Thailand. Every continent contributed to the lunch, but all the food could have been produced and bought locally.

Source: www.ourplanet.com/tunza

Transport accounts for about 13 per cent of global greenhouse gas emissions. Walking or cycling does not create any pollution. It is good for your health and good for the environment. Flying less can also make a huge difference. Aviation is the fastest-growing form of transportation. About 3.5 per cent of greenhouse gases come from air travel. Why not cut down on flying and use trains whenever possible? Every kilometre travelled in a plane produces three times more carbon dioxide per person than travelling by train. Another way of reducing air travel is to buy locally produced food. Buying local means less energy spent on transport and packaging.

Buying less, wasting less

If you buy less, then of course you throw away less. This saves natural resources and energy and also reduces pollution. How many of the things you buy do you actually need or use regularly? Think about Christmas, when you want the latest game console. Is the latest console really all that much better than the old one? Will the old one end up on a landfill where it will take centuries to decay? Are styrofoam packing, wrapping paper and ribbons really necessary? Might it not be better to wait a few months and buy a used console on ebay? Remember: it is our personal choices that influence the production of goods.

Recycling helps to reduce pollution. For example, the energy needed to make one new aluminium can is the same as the energy needed to recycle 20 cans. However, recycling only works if we buy products made from recycled materials.

On average, each person in the UK throws out about 9.8 kilogrammes of rubbish each week. In the United States, the equivalent figure is 14.6 kilogrammes. The production of waste per person keeps growing. We are running out of space to bury our rubbish and we pollute the atmosphere by burning it in incinerators. Although our personal rubbish is a small part of the total waste produced on the planet, it is an important part.

We can change the way we buy, use and dispose of products. For example, paper and card fill up about a fifth of our bins. By using both sides of a piece of paper and buying fewer heavily packaged goods, we save trees, we reduce pollution and we produce less waste. Reusing old shopping bags also helps to reduce the massive quantities of plastic bags littering the planet.

Repair, recycle, reuse

The three Rs – repair, recycle and reuse – are good principles to help us reduce pollution. In previous generations, people mended clothes, reused glass bottles and even cleaned tin foil after use. These were seen as valuable materials. We need to adopt these same values today.

A woman displays a recycled shopping bag made from old clothes. She was selling the bags at a 'creative bazaar' promoting environmental awareness in Wuhan, Hubei Province, China, in May 2008. Recycling can only work if we are prepared to buy products made from recycled materials.

Today, clothes are cheap and are often worn only for as long as they are fashionable. Yet the clothes we buy have a major impact on the environment. Toxic chemicals are sprayed on cotton crops and are used to dye fabrics. Fossil fuels are burned to power textile factories and transport these items around the world.

We can reduce the environmental impact of the clothing industry by thinking about the three Rs. Old clothes can be passed on to younger siblings. They can be repaired or given to a charity shop for people who need them. They can be recycled into new clothes, saving energy and reducing both pollution and the pressure to harvest and mine new natural resources. Today you can buy cotton t-shirts that can be composted, fleeces made from old plastic bottles and belts made from old tyres.

Schoolchildren celebrate Earth Day in Los Angeles, California. Find out about Earth Day and plan a special event to raise awareness of the importance of conserving the earth.

Protecting water

We can help to protect our water resources by thinking about what we pour down the drain or throw into rivers and streams. About 80 per cent of the pollution in our seas comes from the land. Many products we use in our homes contain toxic substances. These include detergents, washing powders, shampoos, cosmetics and oil-based paints. They can harm both our health and the environment. Yet there are often organic and all-natural alternatives that will do the same job without polluting our drinking water.

If we care about water quality, we should also avoid using pesticides and fertilizers in our gardens, as these toxic substances often end up in local water sources. Also, think carefully about how you dispose of litter, or else your plastic bags and water bottles could end up adding to the Great Pacific Garbage Patch (see page 27).

Making noise

Talk to other people in your family, at school or in the neighbourhood about ways of reducing pollution. If enough people change their shopping habits, it could put pressure on your local supermarket to rethink where they get their food from, how it is packaged and how it is transported. Why not write to your local newspaper about these issues? Find out about groups of concerned citizens hoping to make their voices heard in your area, in your country and in the world.

DEBATE

You are in charge

You are doing the food shopping for the week and you want to help reduce pollution.

- Where will you get your food from?
- How will you get the food to your home?
- What kind of cleaning products will you buy?
- What kind of light bulb will you buy?
- What kind of fruit and vegetables will you buy?
- What kind of red meat, chicken or fish will you buy?
- What kind of shopping bag will you use?
- How will your weekly shopping change if you take into account energy use, farming methods, transport, packaging and pollution?

PLEASE REUSE THIS BOOK

It takes about 17 trees to make one tonne of paper, not to mention large amounts of water, chemicals such as chlorine and sulphur, and energy. So please share this book with others so that many people get to read it.

Glossary

acid rain Rain that contains acid as a result of burning fossil fuels.

atmosphere The layer of gases that surrounds and protects the earth. It is about 700 kilometres thick.

biodegradable Breaks down or rots naturally when attacked by bacteria. Examples include food and garden waste.

cadmium A metallic element found mainly in zinc, copper and lead ores.

carbon monoxide A poisonous gas produced when burning fuel. It is mainly emitted from car exhausts.

CFCs (chlorofluorocarbons) Chemicals used in products like aerosols and refrigerators, which attack the ozone layer

compost A mixture of organic household waste, such as vegetable peelings and brown cardboard, and plants that have decomposed over time. Compost can be used to fertilize the garden.

emissions Gases released into the atmosphere.

fossil fuels Fuels formed over a long period of time from the remains of dead plants and animals buried deep in the earth. The main fossil fuels are coal, oil and natural gas.

global warming The gradual increase in the earth's temperature, which most scientists believe has been caused by polluting gases trapping heat in the atmosphere.

greenhouse effect The natural process by which heat is trapped in the atmosphere. Without it, life could not survive on earth.

greenhouse gases Gases, such as carbon dioxide and methane, that trap the sun's heat and warm the earth. Human activity has increased the amount of these greenhouse gases in the atmosphere. Most scientists believe this has caused global warming.

heavy metal Metallic elements that can be harmful to living things and that tend to build up in the food chain. Heavy metals include chromium, mercury, cadmium, arsenic and lead.

herbicide A chemical designed to kill or weaken weeds.

Industrial Revolution The rapid growth of industry that started in the late 18th century. It was made possible by the invention of power-driven machinery, the development of the factory system and the harnessing of energy from fossil fuels such as coal.

nitrogen oxides Polluting gases formed from nitrogen and emitted when fossil fuels are burnt.

oxygen A colourless, odourless gas found in abundance in the atmosphere. Oxygen is vital for life.

ozone A colourless, gaseous form of oxygen.

ozone layer A layer of ozone high up in the atmosphere, which shields the earth from the harmful ultraviolet rays of the sun.

particulate A substance that consists of separate particles, especially airborne pollution such as soot, dust or fumes.

pesticide A chemical designed to kill bugs and pests.

photosynthesis The process by which plants convert sunlight, water and carbon dioxide into food, oxygen and water. They breathe in carbon dioxide and breathe out oxygen.

plankton Microscopic marine organisms. Some, called zooplankton, are animals. Others, called phytoplankton, are plants.

pollutant Something that contaminates air, soil or water.

power plant A facility where power, especially electricity, is generated.

radiation Energy that is transmitted in the form of rays, waves or particles.

radioactive Describes elements, such as uranium, that emit radiation as they change into other elements.

recycle Use materials that have been used before to make new things.

smog Originally a mixture of smoke and fog. Today, smog is air pollution produced by the reaction of hydrocarbons and nitrogen oxides in the presence of sunlight. It is mainly made up of ozone.

solar energy Energy from the sun, which can be converted into heat or electricity.

sulphur dioxide A polluting gas formed from sulphur, emitted when burning fossil fuels.

synthetic Describes substances and materials that are made by humans and do not occur in nature.

toxic Poisonous to humans and other living things.

ultraviolet rays A type of radiation made by the sun that is harmful to plants, animals and people.

United Nations An organization of nations, formed in 1945 to promote peace, security and international cooperation.

Further Information

Books

Green Files: Polluted Planet by Steve Parker (Heinemann, 2004)

Improving Our Environment: Air Pollution by Jen Green (Wayland, 2007)

Precious Earth: The Polluted Planet by Jen Green (Chrysalis, 2004)

Save the Planet: Fight Air Pollution by Terry Jennings (Chrysalis, 2005)

Understanding Pollution: Acid Rain by Lucy Poddington (Franklin Watts, 2006)

Understanding Pollution: Nuclear Waste by Lucy Poddington (Franklin Watts, 2006)

You Can Save the Planet: Clean Planet: Stopping Litter and Pollution by Tristan Boyer (Heinemann, 2005)

Your Environment: Pollution by Cindy Leany (Franklin Watts, 2007)

Websites

epa.gov/kids
Environmental Kids Club: a site for young people produced by the Environmental Protection Agency, providing facts and action you can take.

www.unep.org/tunza/youth
This website provides information about how young people can engage in environmental activities and the work of the United Nations Environmental Programme.

www.wasteonline.org.uk
Waste Online: a great source of information on every aspect of waste.

www.weeeman.org
The WEEE Man: an initiative to raise awareness of the amount of electrical and electronic waste we produce. The site allows you to measure your own impact.

www.youthxchange.net
YouthXchange: a website full of information from all around the world about reducing consumption and waste.

www.globalcool.org
Tips on how to use and lose less energy by doing many easy things.

Debate Panel Answers

Page 11: Many people and organizations support the principle that polluters should pay. In other words, whoever causes pollution has to pay to clean it up. Businesses should pay for the disposal of the packaging and waste they create. Oil companies should pay for cleaning up spills. We, as consumers, should pay for the pollution and waste that we produce. If businesses and individuals know they will have to pay for the pollution they create, they are less likely to pollute in future. Nevertheless it is a good idea to pressure governments to set standards and guidelines so people know what actions they should take to minimize pollution.

Page 19: Today, most scientists agree that burning fossil fuel is responsible for global warming. However, there are different views about how we need to tackle the issue. Many people believe that the best plan for the future would be a combination of renewable energy and cleaner technologies. Nuclear energy does not generate air pollution but is dangerous. It produces toxic waste which can be dangerous for thousands of years. Finding ways of reducing our energy use is also a good idea.

Page 27: Oil spills can have a devastating effect on the environment. Oil companies are usually held responsible and asked to pay a fine. The company responsible for the *Exxon Valdez* oil spill was initially required to pay five billion US dollars. But in June 2008, the fine was reduced to a tenth of the original sum. So do fines really work? A key problem is that the fuels we use for energy are extracted in places far away from where the energy is eventually used. Maybe we need to look at ways of finding local energy sources, closer to where people live.

Page 33: The disposal of mobile phones and other electronic items produce a huge amount of pollution because of the different materials and toxic components used to make these products. When recycling your mobile phone, you need to make sure that you deal with responsible recyclers. To find out about schemes in your local area, you can look at directories on the Internet.

Page 39: Mimicking nature means using nature as a model in the way we use natural resources and design things. In nature, everything is interconnected and materials are used and reused over and over again. So when you design your house, ask yourself: 'How does nature perform this function without creating any waste or pollution?' Try to use materials that can be composted or recycled. Try to avoid using toxic substances that pollute the environment and are often not necessary. Think about the natural water cycle and how to get water from the soil and collect rainwater. Think about possible renewable sources of energy and how the shape of your house could help retain heat in cold weather or keep cool in hot weather.

Page 45: As a general rule, try to think about where your food comes from and how it has been produced. Did it have to travel miles to reach you or was it produced locally? Was it grown in season or produced in greenhouses, consuming lots of electricity? Was it produced with the use of chemical fertilizers and pesticides or grown organically? Check the labels to find out. Is the packaging necessary and, if so, is it made of materials that can be recycled or composted? One way of easily reducing pollution is to buy local produce from a farmers' market. Home delivery is also becoming more popular in many countries and helps to cut down on car dependence. And remember, you can make your voice heard by asking your local supermarket to stock more local organic produce.

Index

Page numbers in **bold** refer to illustrations and charts.